U2 THE BEST OF 1980-1990

Contents

Exclusive Distributors:
Music Sales Limited
8/9 Frith Street,
London W1V 5TZ, England.
Music Sales Pty Limited
120 Rothschild Avenue
Rosebery, NSW 2018,
Australia.

Order No.AM957022
ISBN 0-7119-7309-1
This book © Copyright 1999 by Wise Publications
www.musicsales.com

Unauthorised reproduction of any part of this publication by any
means including photocopying is an infringement of copyright.

New music arrangements by Martin Shellard
New music processed by Digital Music Art
Design by Averill Brophy Associates, Dublin

This publication is not authorised for sale
in the United States of America and/or Canada.

Wise Publications
London/New York/Sydney/Paris/Copenhagen/Madrid

Your Guarantee of Quality
As publishers, we strive to produce every book to the highest
commercial standards. Whilst endeavouring to retain the original
running order of the recorded album, the book has been
carefully designed to minimise
awkward page turns and to make playing from it a real
pleasure. Particular care has been given to specifying acid-
free, neutral-sized paper made from pulps which have not
been elemental chlorine bleached. This pulp is from farmed
sustainable forests and was produced with special regard
for the environment. Throughout, the printing and binding
have been planned to ensure a sturdy, attractive publication
which should give years of enjoyment. If your copy fails to
meet our high standards, please inform us and we will
gladly replace it.

Music Sales' complete catalogue describes thousands of
titles and is available in full colour sections by subject,
direct from Music Sales Limited. Please state your areas of
interest and send a cheque/postal order for £1.50 for
postage to: Music Sales Limited, Newmarket Road,
Bury St. Edmunds, Suffolk IP33 3YB.

PRIDE (In The Name Of Love)

Words & Music by U2

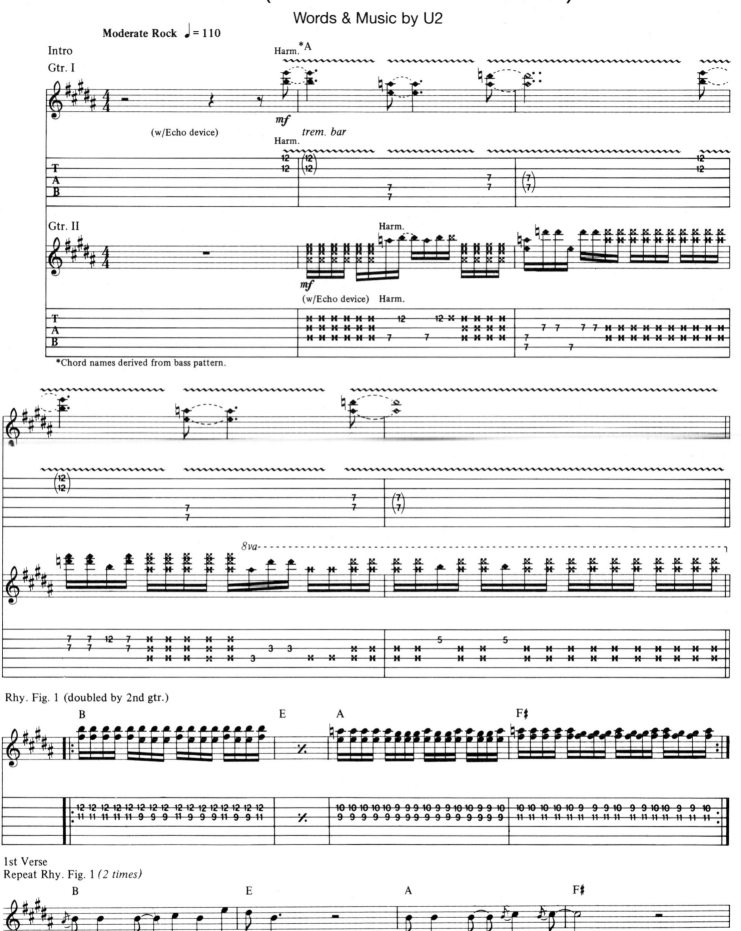

*Chord names derived from bass pattern.

One man   come__ in the name of love,   one man   come__ and   go.__

Chorus
w/Rhy. Fig. 1 (2 times)

One man come he to jus-ti-fy, one man to o-ver-throw. In the name

of love, what more in the name of love. In the name

of love, what more in the name of love.

2nd Verse

One man caught on a barbed wive fence, one man he re-sist.

Gtr. I   Rhy. Fig. 2

sustain all notes

Gtr. II   Rhy. Fig 2A

sustain all notes

†Played by the bass only.

One man washed on an emp-ty beach, one man be-trayed with a kiss. In the name

3

NEW YEAR'S DAY

Words & Music by U2

Am   C   Em

2.

Says it's true

Harm. — — — — — — — '   Harm. — — — '

Bridge

G⁵   A⁵

— that it's true, _____ and we can break _____ through, _____ though—

G⁵   Fsus²

torn   in   two, _____ we can be____ one. _____

Chorus

G⁵   A⁵

I, _____ I will be - gin a - gain,

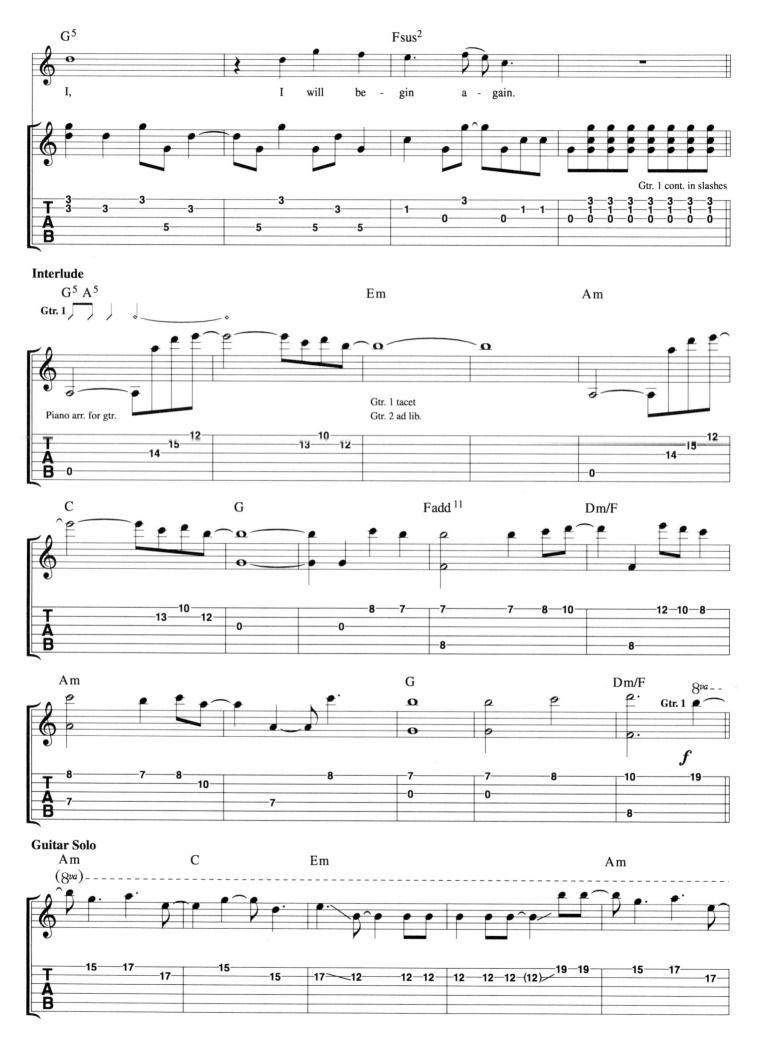

WITH OR WITHOUT YOU

Words & Music by U2

* Gtr. III notes sound 1 octave higher than written.

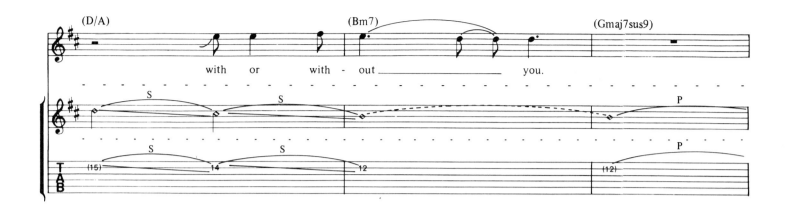

(D/A)   (Bm7)   (Gmaj7sus9)

with or with - out _____ you.

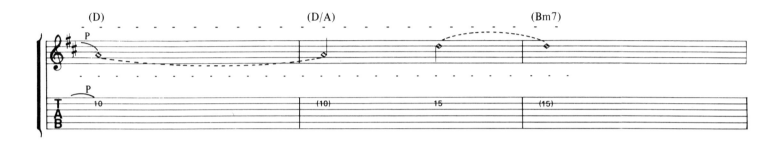

(D)   (D/A)   (Bm7)

Continue Rhy. Fig. 1A

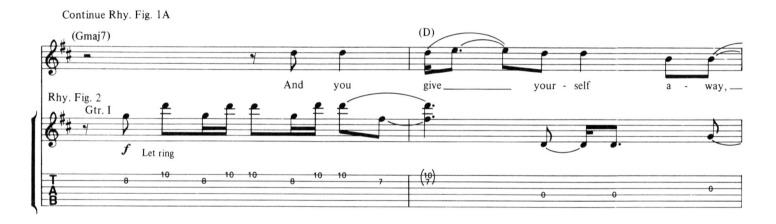

(Gmaj7)   (D)

And you give _____ your - self a - way,

Rhy. Fig. 2
Gtr. I

f   Let ring

Repeat Rhy. Fig. 2 (until change)

(D/A)   (Bm7)   (Gmaj7)

_____ and you give _____ your - self a - way, _____ and you give, _____

(D)   (D/A)   (Bm7)

_____ and you give, _____ and you give _____ your - self a - way. _____

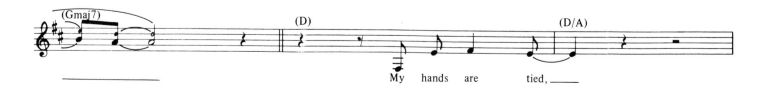

(Gmaj7)   (D)   (D/A)

_____ My hands are tied, _____

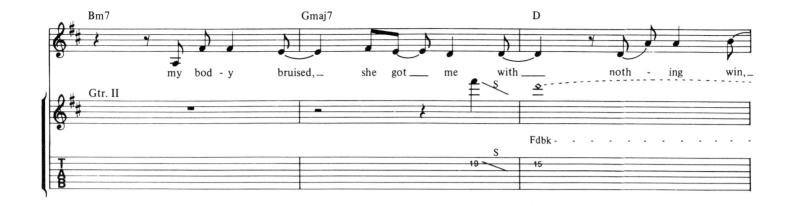

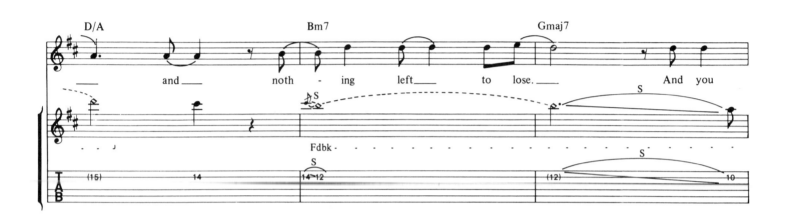

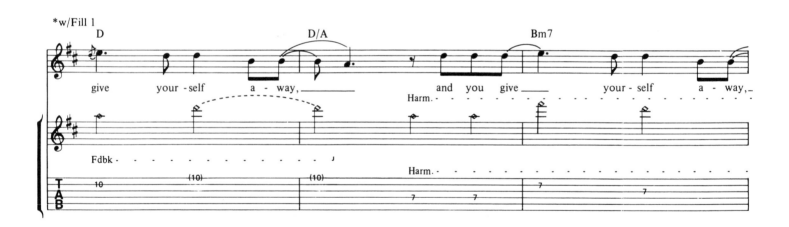

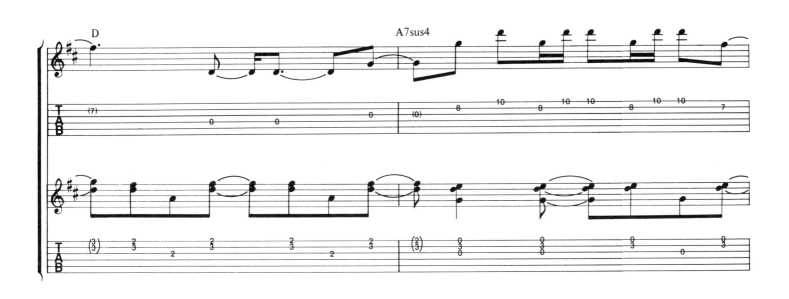

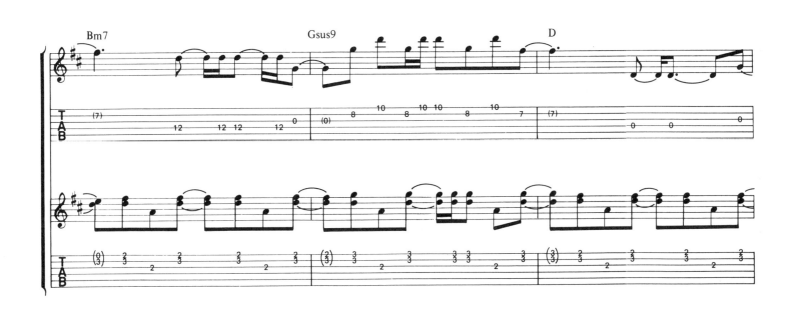

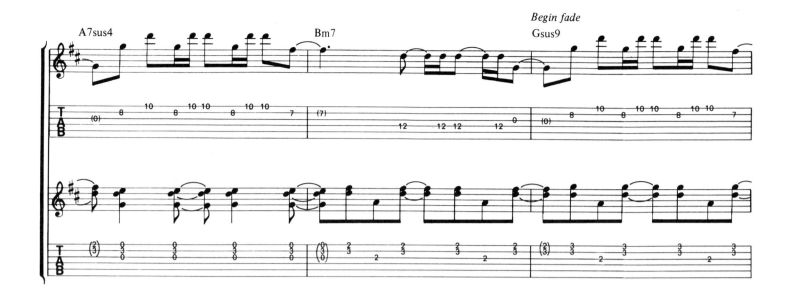

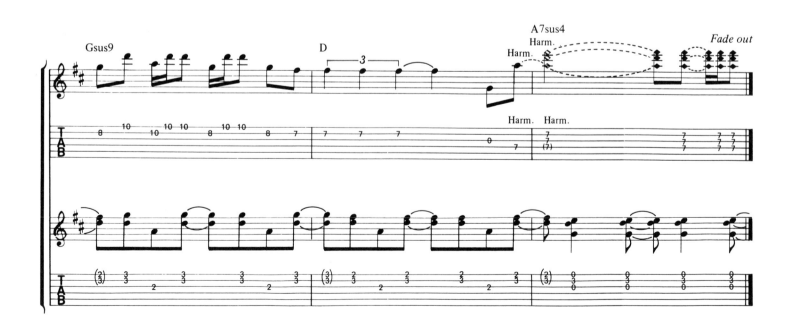

22

I STILL HAVEN'T FOUND WHAT I'M LOOKING FOR

Words & Music by U2

* Use distortion.

* Parenthesized chords refer to tabbed guitar.

2nd Verse
w/Rhy. Fig. 1
Rhy. Fig. 2   w/Rhy. Fill 1   Resume Rhy. Fig. 1 until Chorus

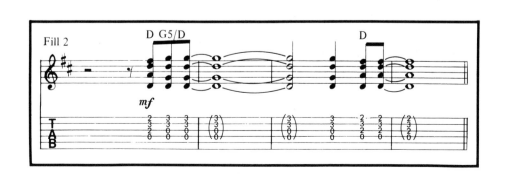

* Use max. echo for fills 1 - 4.

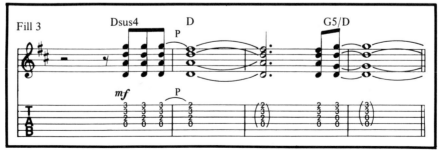

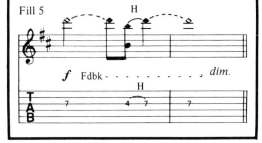

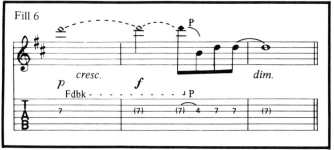

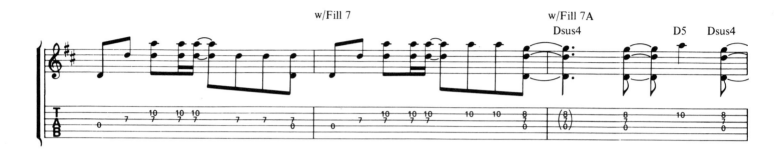

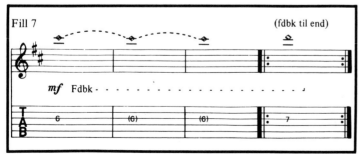

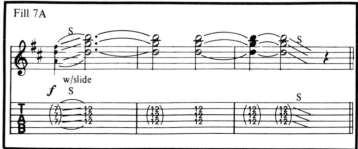

SUNDAY BLOODY SUNDAY

Words & Music by U2

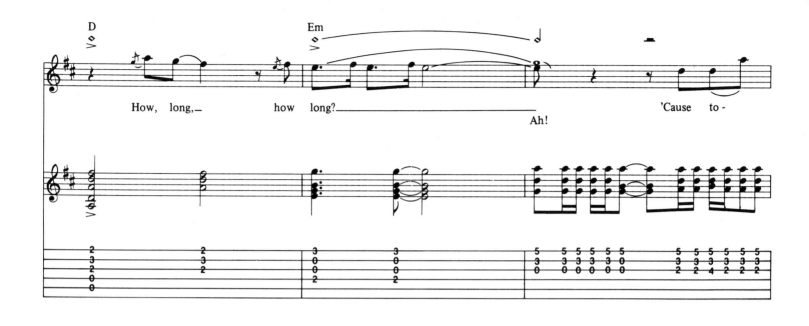

How, long,— how long?_____ 'Cause to-

Ah!

night we can be as one,— to-night!

Ah._____ Ah,— ah.

Elec. gtr. (doubled by
12 stg. acoustic)

Harm. *(15ma)* Harm. *(15ma)*

Harm. *(15ma)*

Harm. Harm. Harm.

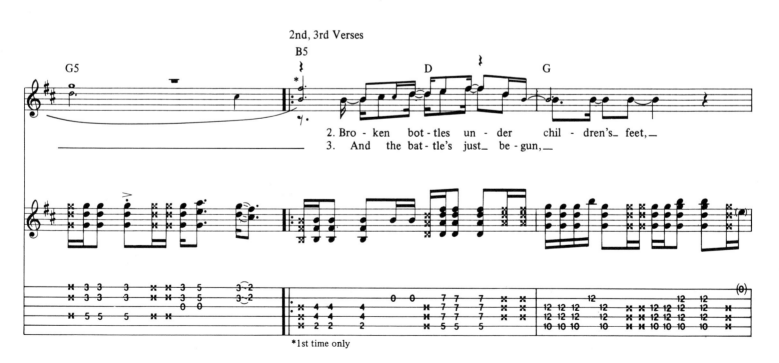

2nd, 3rd Verses

2. Bro - ken bot - tles un - der chil - dren's_ feet,—
3. And the bat - tle's just_ be - gun,—

*1st time only

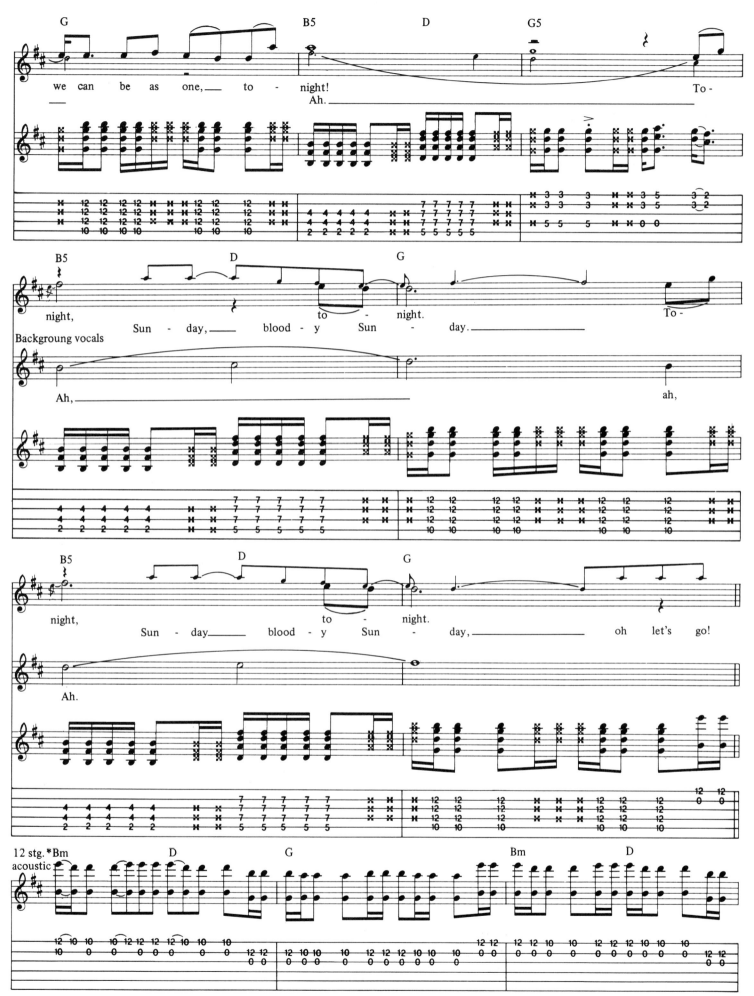

*Chord names derived from bass pattern.

BAD

Words & Music by U2

Interlude

41

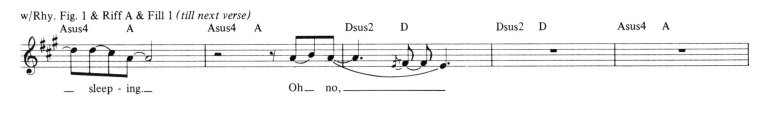

w/Rhy. Fig. 1 & Riff A & Fill 1 *(till next verse)*

_ sleep - ing._   Oh_ no,_____

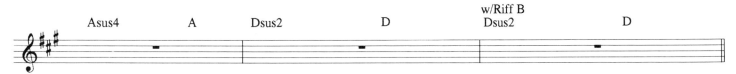

w/Riff B

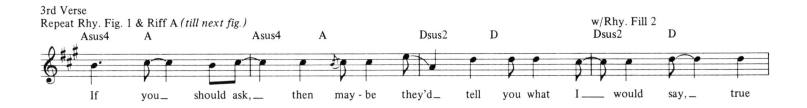

3rd Verse
Repeat Rhy. Fig. 1 & Riff A *(till next fig.)*   w/Rhy. Fill 2

If   you_   should ask,_   then   may - be   they'd_   tell   you what   I __ would   say,_   true

Resume Rhy. Fig. 1

col - ors   fly_   in   blue and   black,_   bruised   silk - en   sky,_   and   burn - ing   flag._

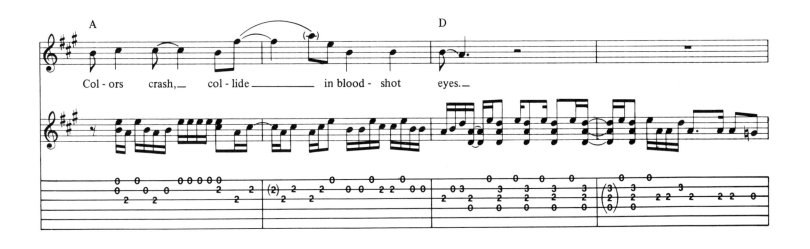

Col - ors   crash,_   col - lide _____ in blood - shot   eyes._

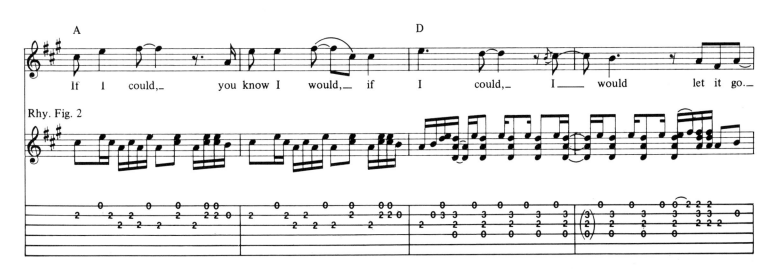

If   I   could,_   you know I   would,_   if   I   could,_   I __ would   let it go._

Rhy. Fig. 2

This des - per - a - tion,— dis - lo -

ca - tion,— sep - a - ra - tion,— con - dem - na - tion,— rev - e -

D.S. al Coda

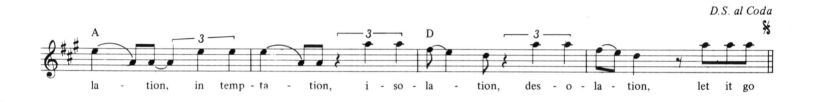

la - tion, in temp - ta - tion, i - so - la - tion, des - o - la - tion, let it go

Coda

Begin fade

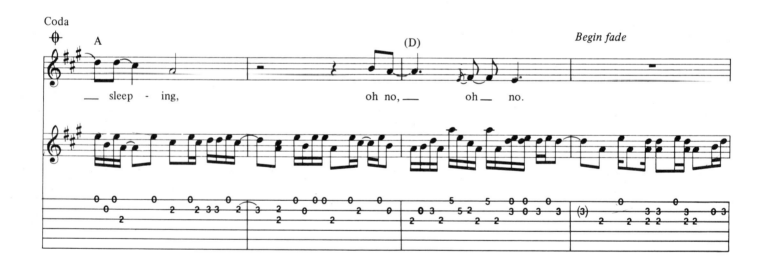

— sleep - ing, oh no, — oh — no.

Fade out

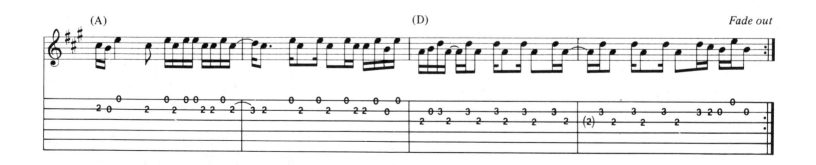

44

WHERE THE STREETS HAVE NO NAME

Words & Music by U2

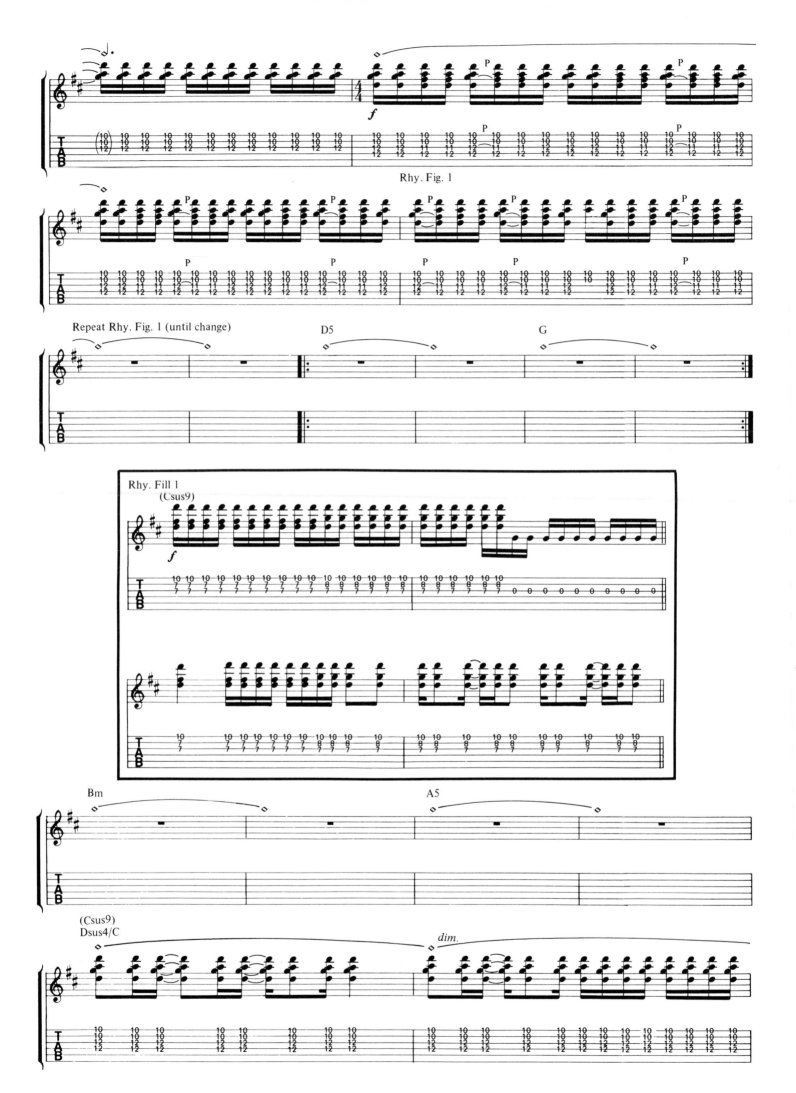

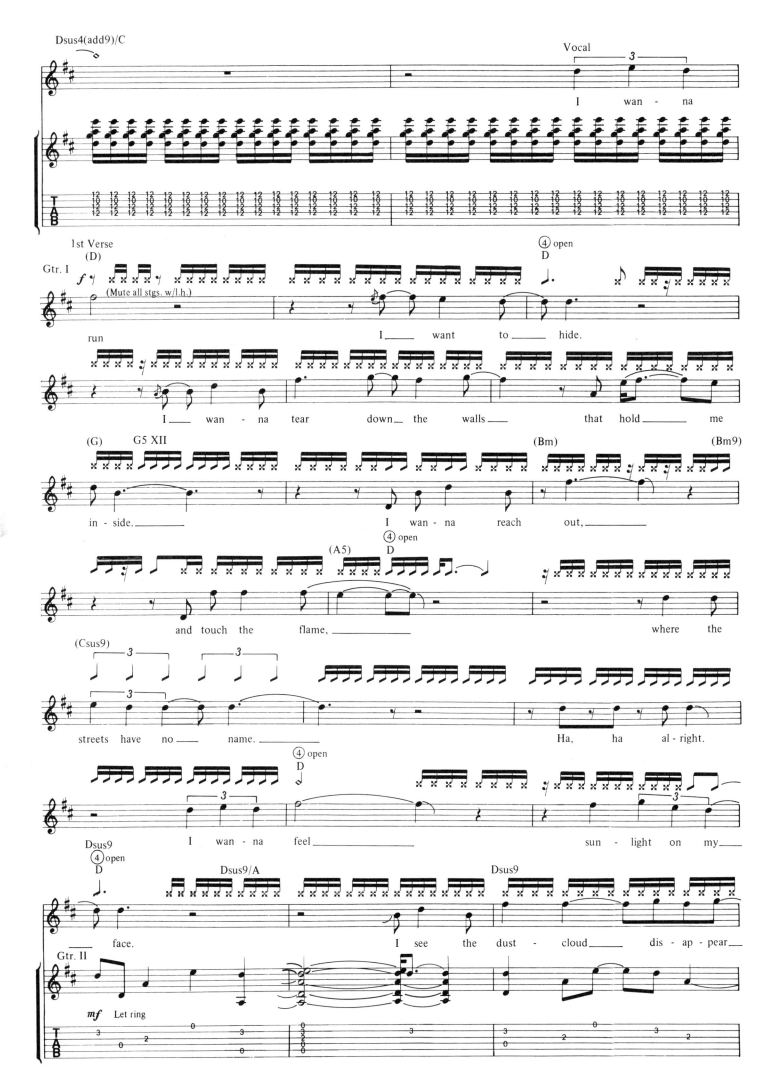

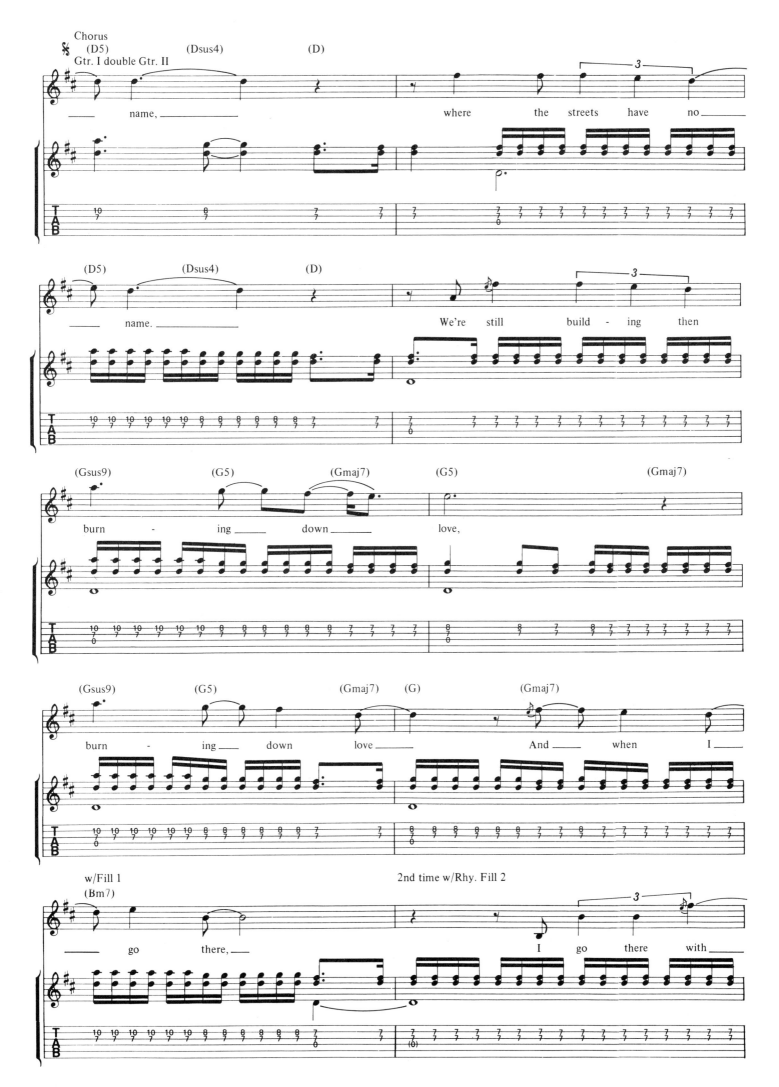

50

I WILL FOLLOW

Words & Music by U2

but it's your eyes.___ Hey! Yeah!___ Your___

Repeat Rhy. Fig. 1 *(2 times)*

N.C. (E5) (A) (E5) (A) (D)

— eyes,_____ oh!_____ w/Rhy. Fill 1

(E5) (A) (E5) (A) (D)

You can

Chorus

E5 A(7sus4) E5 A(7sus4)

walk a-way, walk a-way, walk a-way, walk a-way, I___ will fol-low if you

E5 A(7sus4) E5

walk a-way, walk a-way, walk a-way, walk a-way, I___ will fol-

Rhy. Fill 1

THE UNFORGETTABLE FIRE

Words & Music by U2

62

*Low stgs. only
†High stgs. only

(w/slide)

(w/o slide)
Let ring

(B♭)

(Strings arr. for gtr.)

SWEETEST THING

Words & Music by U2

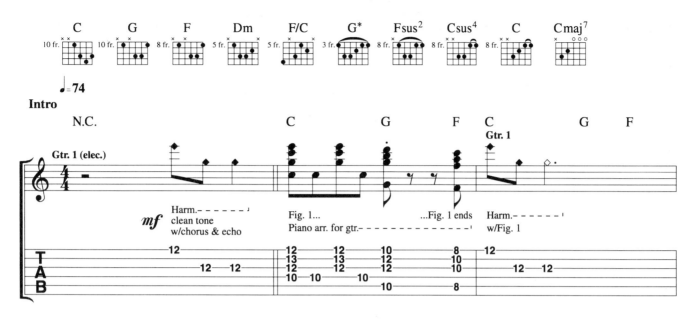

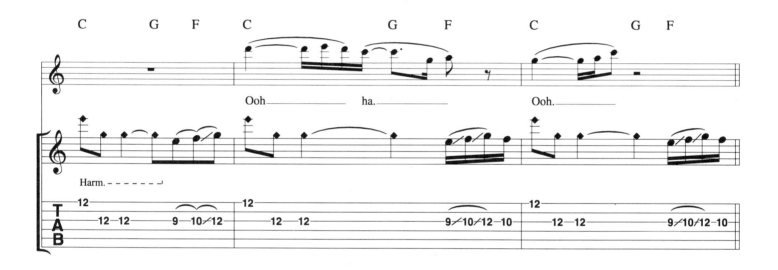

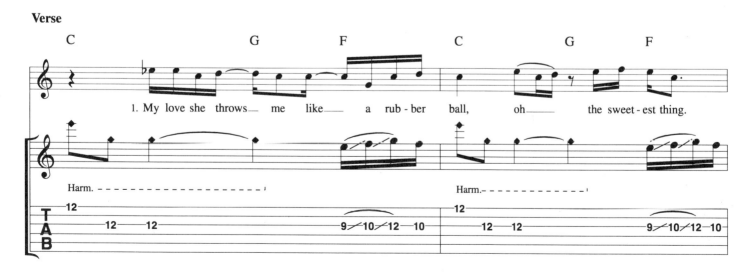

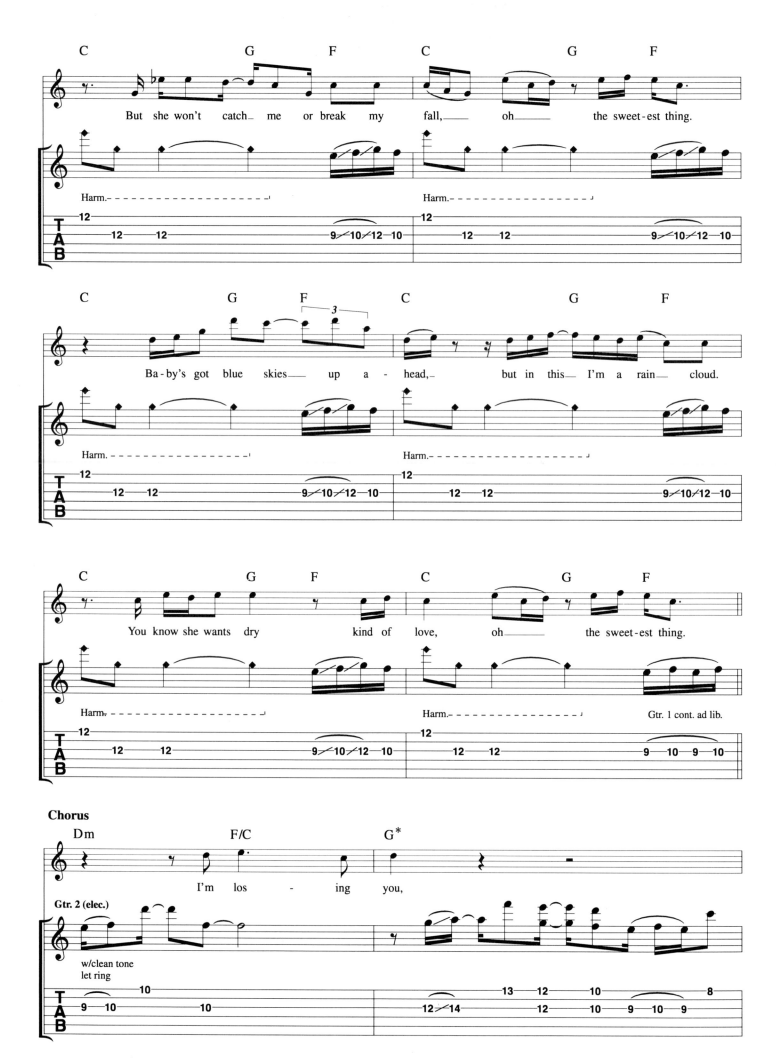

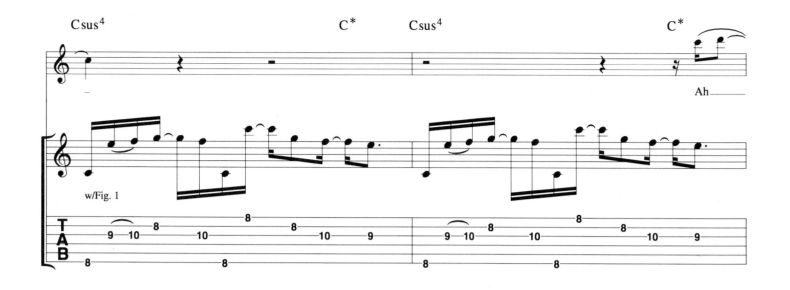

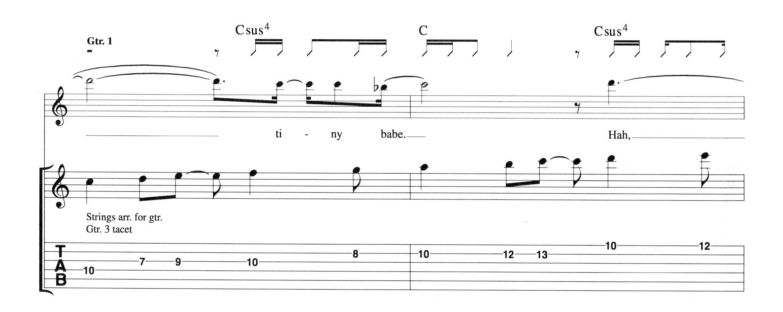

Verse

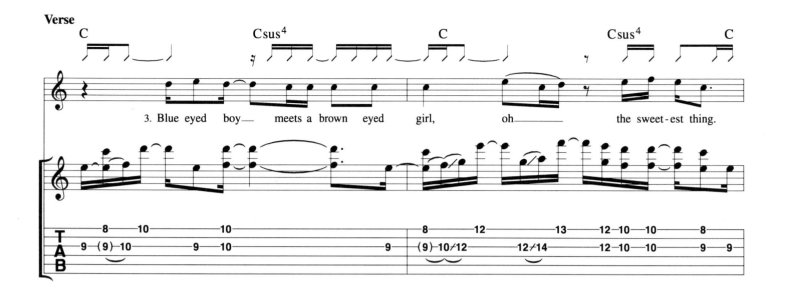

3. Blue eyed boy— meets a brown eyed girl, oh——— the sweet-est thing.

You could sew it up— but you still see the tear, oh——— the sweet-est thing.

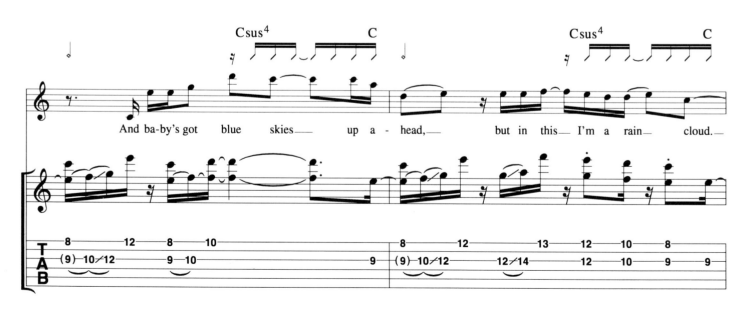

And ba-by's got blue skies— up a - head,— but in this— I'm a rain— cloud.—

DESIRE

Words & Music by U2

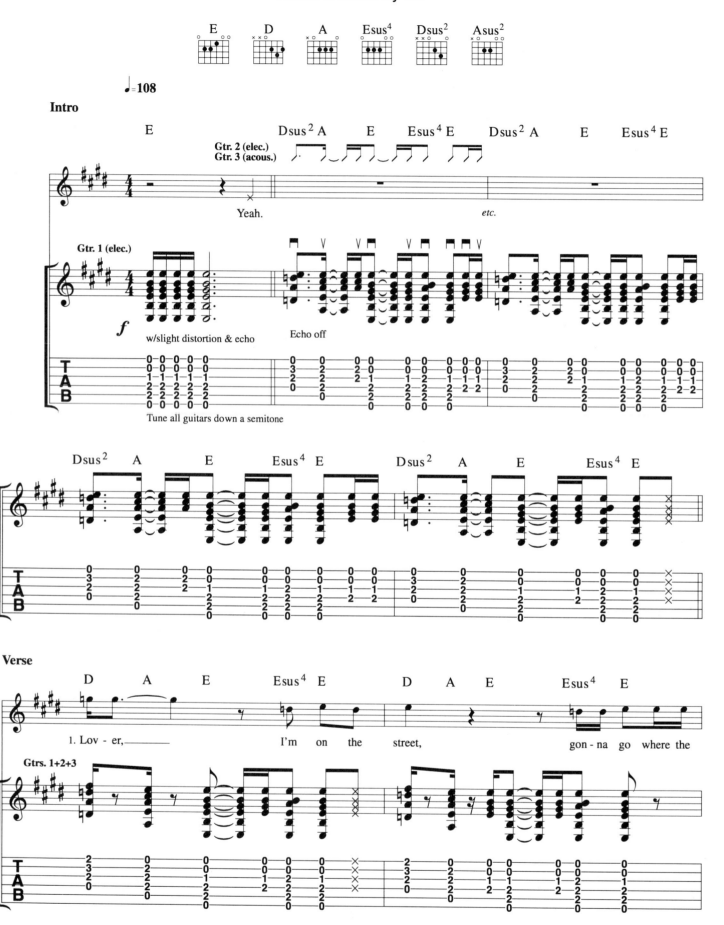

Chorus

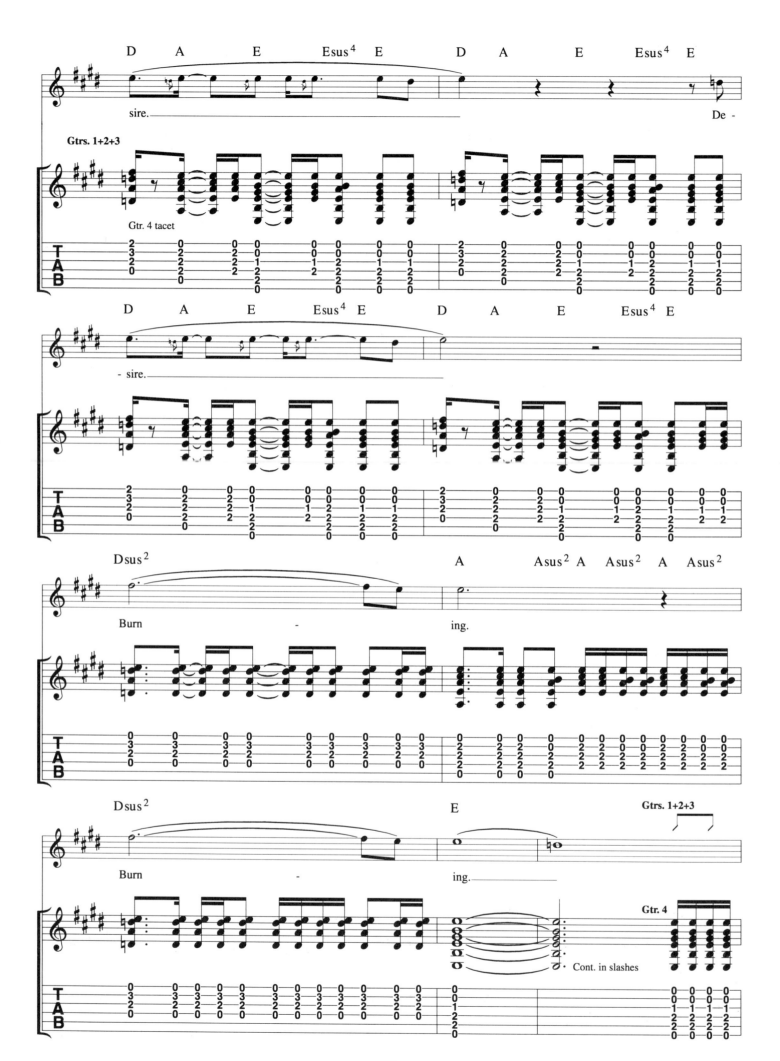

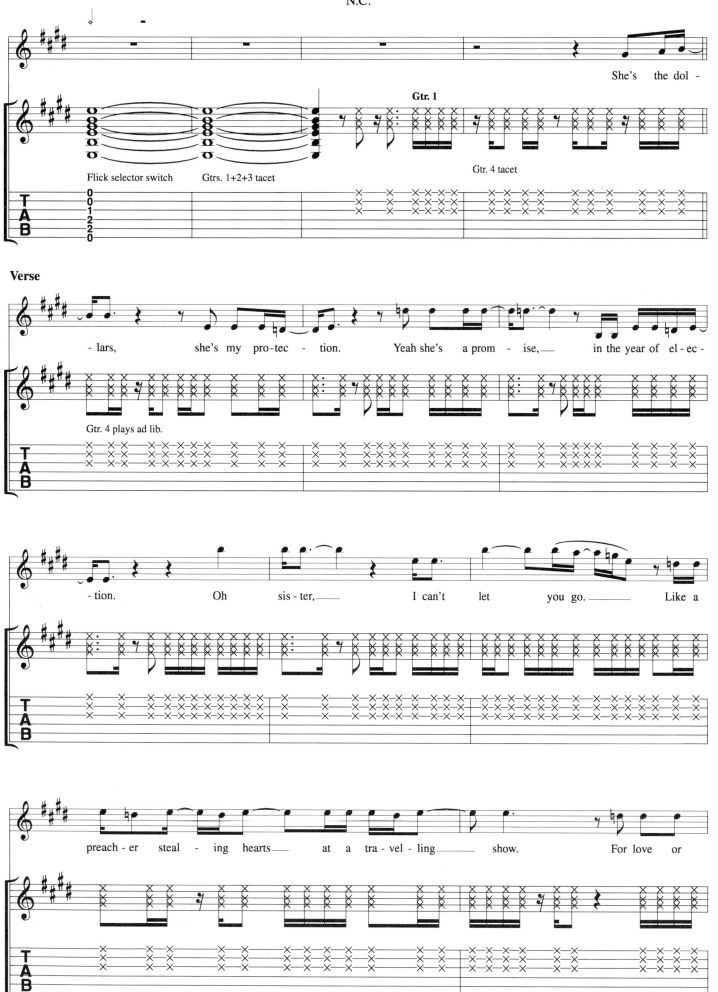

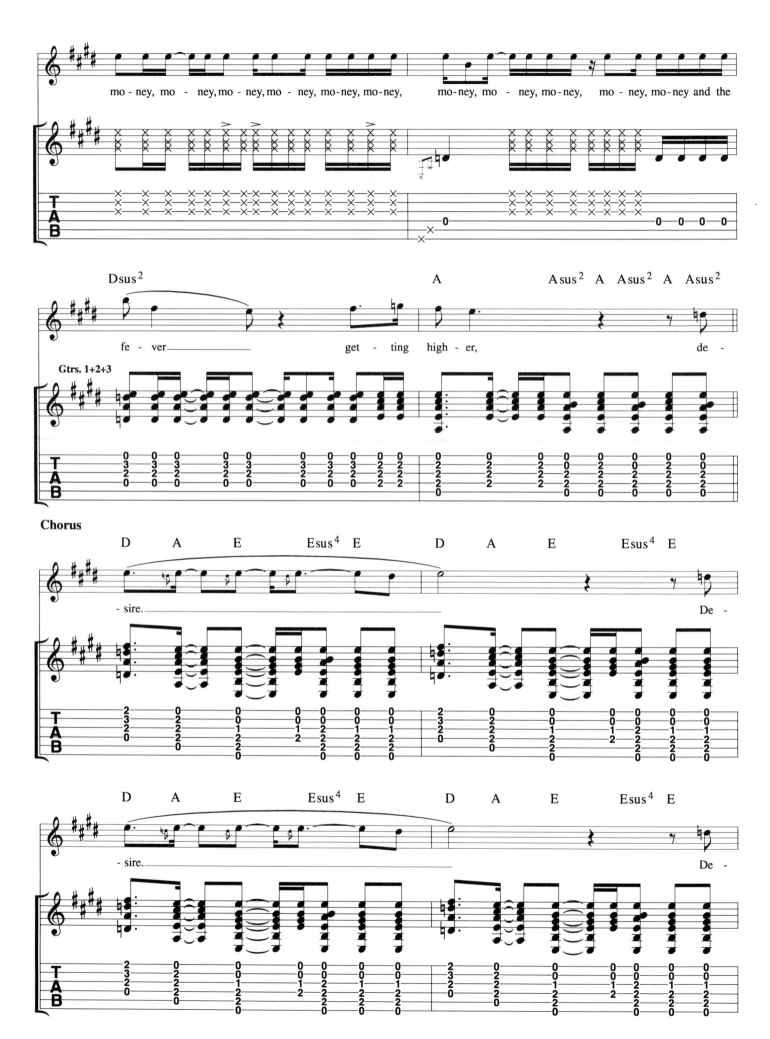

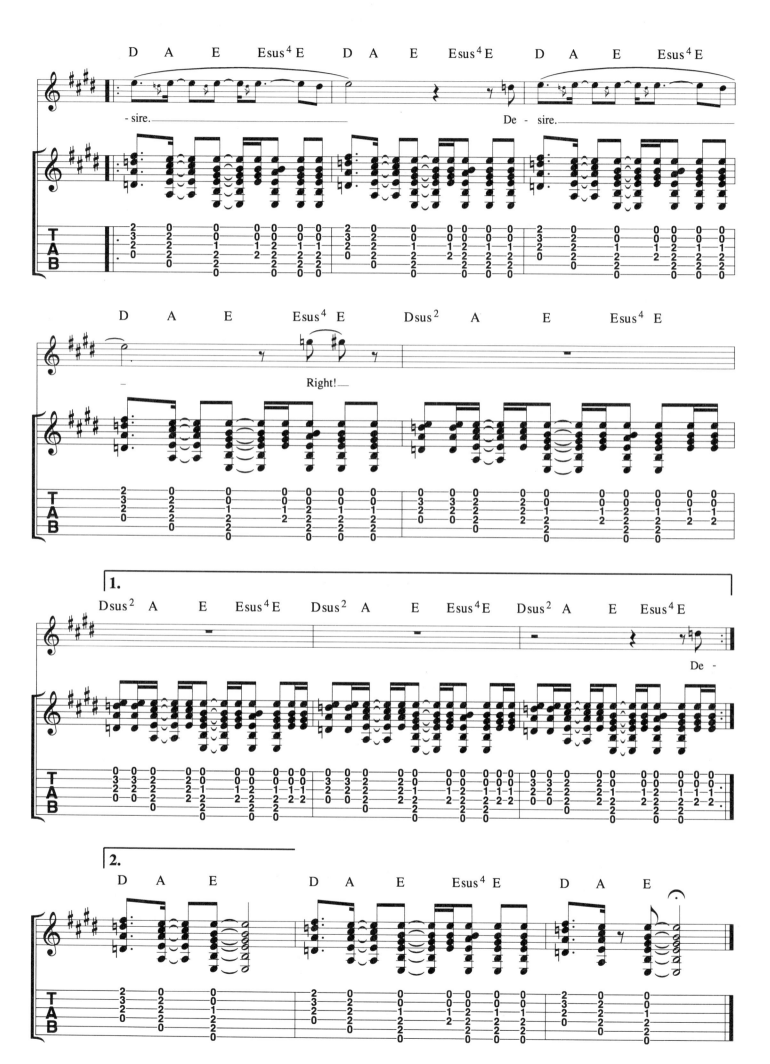

WHEN LOVE COMES TO TOWN

Words & Music by U2

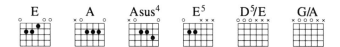

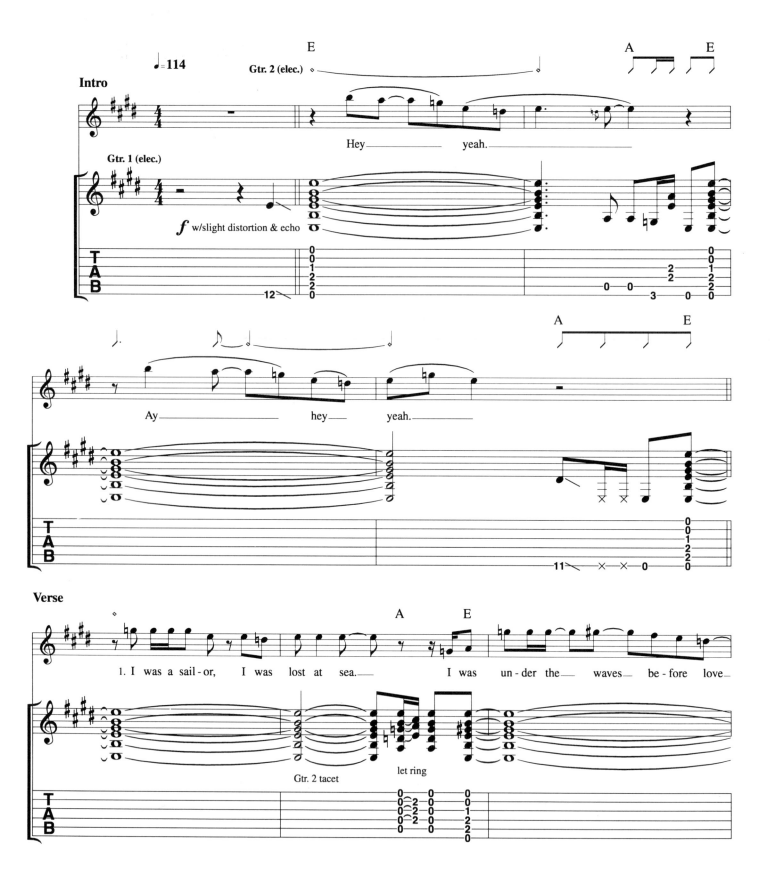

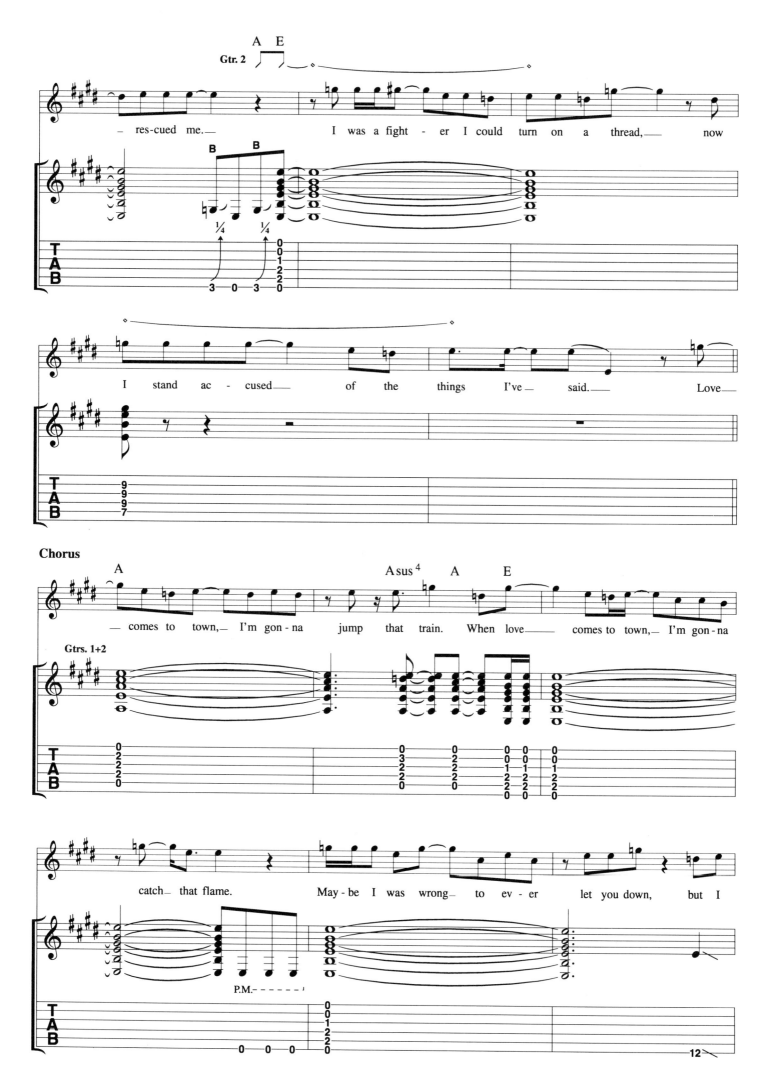

did what I did be - fore love___ came to town.

+echo

cont. in slashes

w/dist.

Verse

2. Used to make___ love___ un - der a red___ sun - set, I was mak - ing pro - mi - ses I would

Gtr. 3 tacet

soon for - get.___ She was pale as the lace___ of her___

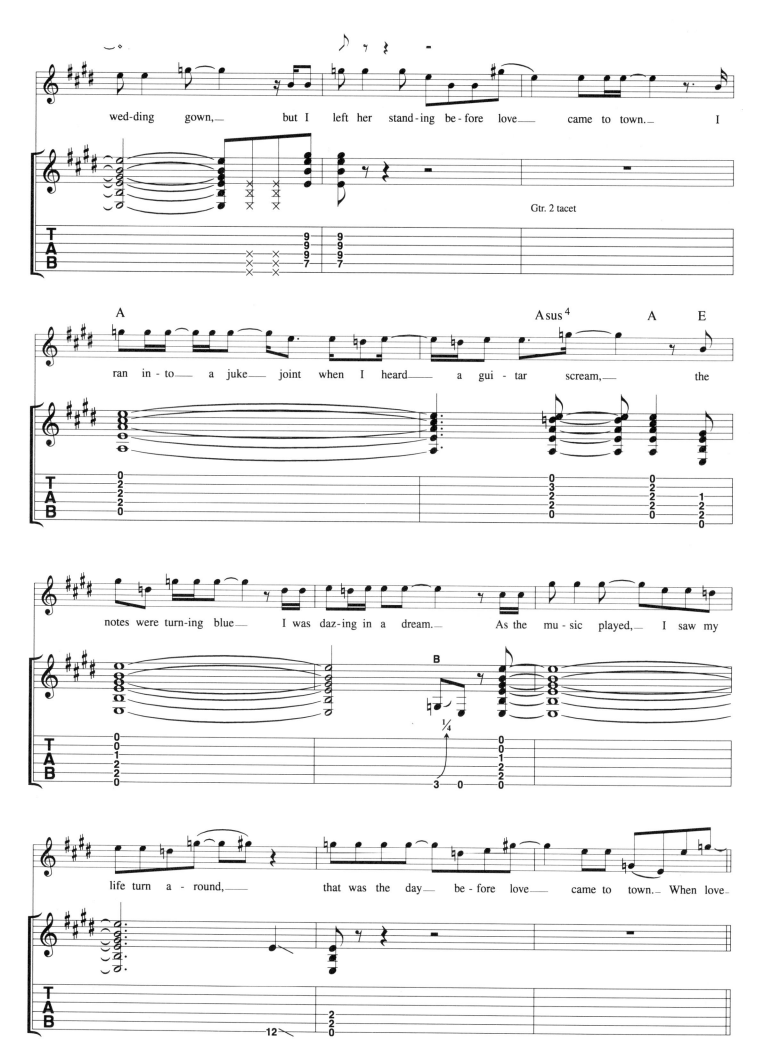

wed-ding gown,— but I left her stand-ing be-fore love— came to town.— I

Gtr. 2 tacet

A   Asus⁴   A   E

ran in-to a juke— joint when I heard— a gui-tar scream,— the

notes were turn-ing blue— I was daz-ing in a dream. As the mu-sic played,— I saw my

life turn a-round,— that was the day— be-fore love— came to town.— When love—

Chorus

86

Chorus

Guitar Solo

Outro

ANGEL OF HARLEM

Words & Music by U2

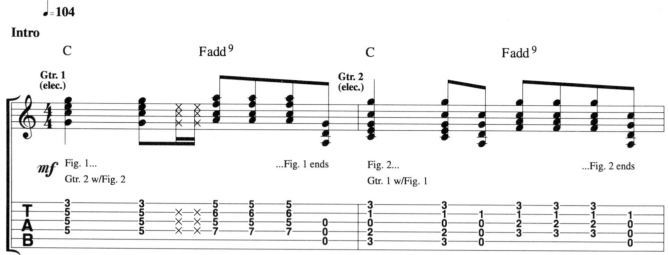

♩ = 104

Intro

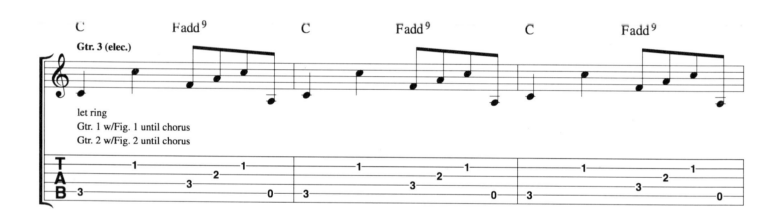

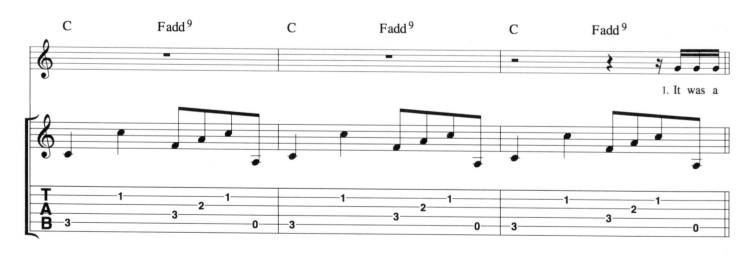

1. It was a

Verse

Verse

3. Blue light on the av-en-ue, God knows they got to you. An

emp-ty glass a la-dy sings, Eyes swol - len like a bee sting.

Blind - ed, you lost your way, through side streets and the al - ley way like a

star ex - plo - ding in the night, fall-ing to the ci - ty in broad day - light.

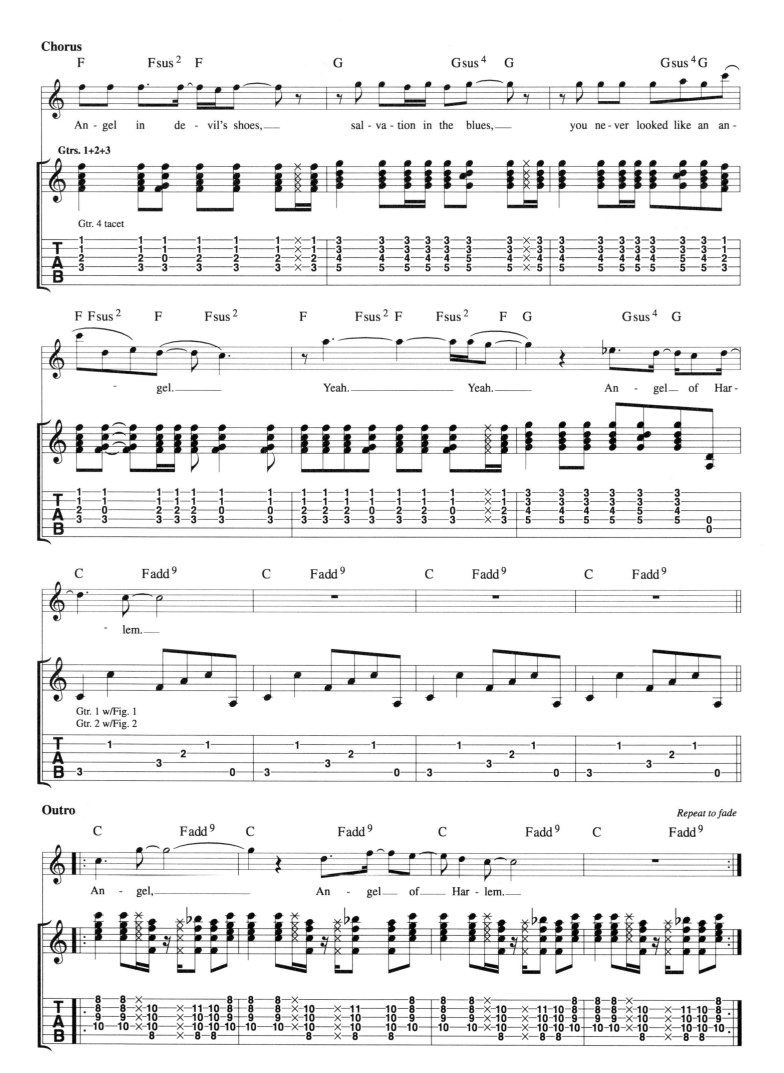

ALL I WANT IS YOU

Words & Music by U2

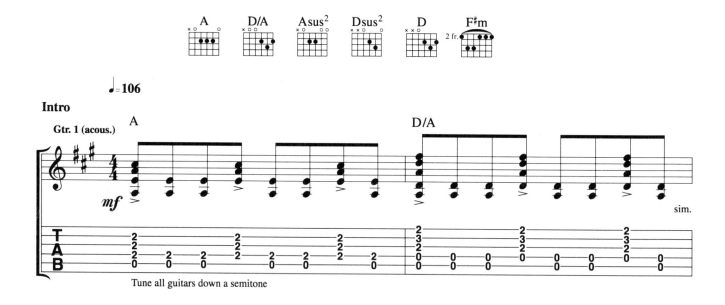

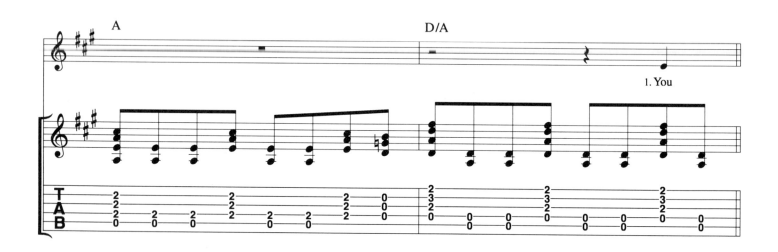

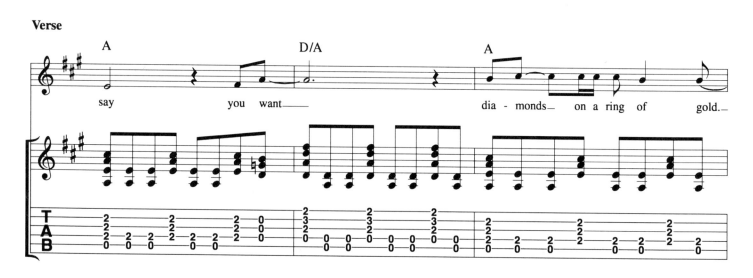

Chorus

Verse

Chorus

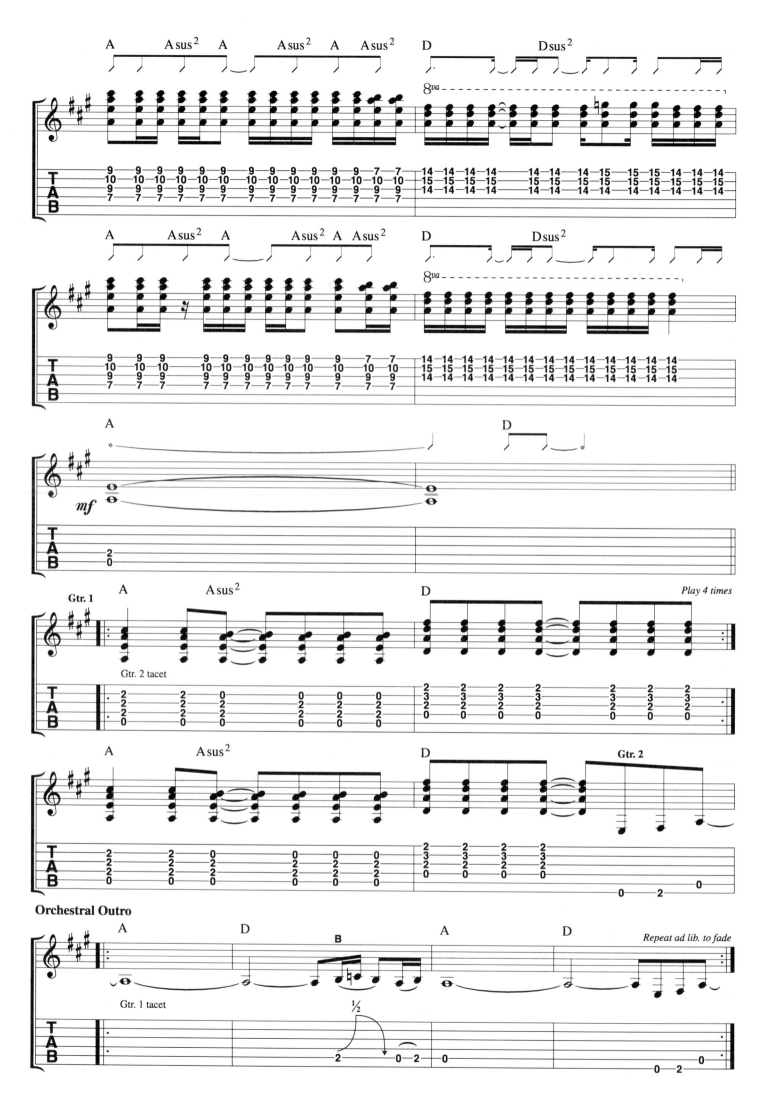

Orchestral Outro

Guitar Tablature Explained

Guitar music can be notated three different ways: on a musical stave, in tablature, and in rhythm slashes

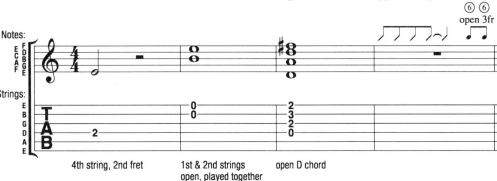

RHYTHM SLASHES are written above the stave. Strum chords in the rhythm indicated. Round noteheads indicate single notes.

THE MUSICAL STAVE shows pitches and rhythms and is divided by lines into bars. Pitches are named after the first seven letters of the alphabet.

TABLATURE graphically represents the guitar fingerboard. Each horizontal line represents a string, and each number represents a fret.

4th string, 2nd fret

1st & 2nd strings open, played together

open D chord

definitions for special guitar notation

SEMI-TONE BEND: Strike the note and bend up a semi-tone (1/2 step).

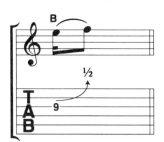

WHOLE-TONE BEND: Strike the note and bend up a whole-tone (whole step).

GRACE NOTE BEND: Strike the note and bend as indicated. Play the first note as quickly as possible.

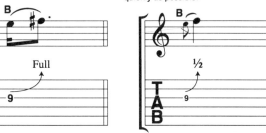

QUARTER-TONE BEND: Strike the note and bend up a 1/4 step.

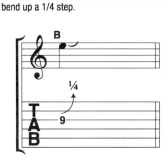

BEND & RELEASE: Strike the note and bend up as indicated, then release back to the original note.

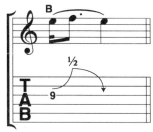

BEND & RESTRIKE: Strike the note and bend as indicated then restrike the string where the symbol occurs.

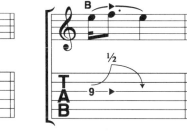

PRE-BEND: Bend the note as indicated, then strike it.

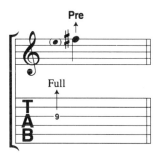

PRE-BEND & RELEASE: Bend the note as indicated. Strike it and release the note back to the original pitch.

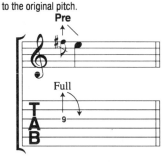

HAMMER-ON: Strike the first (lower) note with one finger, then sound the higher note (on the same string) with another finger by fretting it without picking.

PULL-OFF: Place both fingers on the notes to be sounded. Strike the first note and without picking, pull the finger off to sound the second (lower) note.

LEGATO SLIDE (GLISS): Strike the first note and then slide the same fret-hand finger up or down to the second note. The second note is not struck.

SHIFT SLIDE (GLISS & RESTRIKE): Same as legato slide, except the second note is struck.

NATURAL HARMONIC: Strike the note while the fret-hand lightly touches the string directly over the fret indicated.

PICK SCRAPE: The edge of the pick is rubbed down (or up) the string, producing a scratchy sound.

PALM MUTING: The note is partially muted by the pick hand lightly touching the string(s) just before the bridge.

MUFFLED STRINGS: A percussive sound is produced by laying the fret hand across the string(s) without depressing, and striking them with the pick hand.

NOTE: The speed of any bend is indicated by the music notation and tempo.

Présentation De La Tablature De Guitare

Il existe trois façons différentes de noter la musique pour guitare : à l'aide d'une portée musicale, de tablatures ou de barres rythmiques.

Les BARRES RYTHMIQUES sont indiquées au-dessus de la portée. Jouez les accords dans le rythme indiqué. Les notes rondes indiquent des notes réciles.

La PORTÉE MUSICALE indique les notes et rythmes et est divisée en mesures. Cette division est représentée par des lignes. Les notes sont : do, ré, mi, fa, sol, la, si.

La PORTÉE EN TABLATURE est une représentation graphique des touches de guitare. Chaque ligne horizontale correspond à une corde et chaque chiffre correspond à une case.

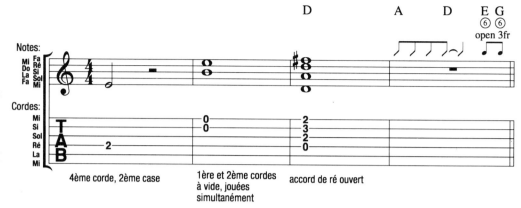

4ème corde, 2ème case   1ère et 2ème cordes à vide, jouées simultanément   accord de ré ouvert

Notation Spéciale De Guitare : Définitions

TIRÉ DEMI-TON : Jouez la note et tirez la corde afin d'élever la note d'un demi-ton (étape à moitié).

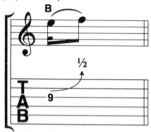

TIRÉ PLEIN : Jouez la note et tirez la corde afin d'élever la note d'un ton entier (étape entière).

TIRÉ D'AGRÉMENT : Jouez la note et tirez la corde comme indiqué. Jouez la première note aussi vite que possible.

TIRÉ QUART DE TON : Jouez la note et tirez la corde afin d'élever la note d'un quart de ton.

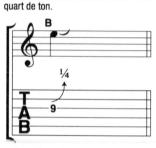

TIRÉ ET LÂCHÉ : Jouez la note et tirez la corde comme indiqué, puis relâchez, afin d'obtenir de nouveau la note de départ.

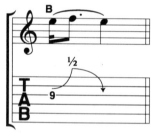

TIRÉ ET REJOUÉ : Jouez la note et tirez la corde comme indiqué puis rejouez la corde où le symbole apparaît.

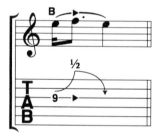

PRÉ-TIRÉ : Tirez la corde comme indiqué puis jouez cette note.

PRÉ-TIRÉ ET LÂCHÉ : Tirez la corde comme indiqué. Jouez la note puis relâchez la corde afin d'obtenir le ton de départ.

HAMMER-ON: Jouez la première note (plus basse) avec un doigt puis jouez la note plus haute sur la même corde avec un autre doigt, sur le manche mais sans vous servir du médiator.

PULL-OFF: Positionnez deux doigts sur les notes à jouer. Jouez la première note et sans vous servir du médiator, dégagez un doigt pour obtenir la deuxième note, plus basse.

GLISSANDO : Jouez la première note puis faites glisser le doigt le long du manche pour obtenir la seconde note qui, elle, n'est pas jouée.

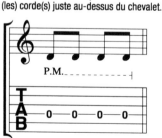

GLISSANDO ET REJOUÉ : Identique au glissando à ceci près que la seconde note est jouée.

HARMONIQUES NATURELLES : Jouez la note tandis qu'un doigt effleure la corde sur le manche correspondant à la case indiquée.

PICK SCRAPE (SCRATCH) : On fait glisser le médiator le long de la corde, ce qui produit un son éraillé.

ÉTOUFFÉ DE LA PAUME : La note est partiellement étouffée par la main (celle qui se sert du médiator). Elle effleure la (les) corde(s) juste au-dessus du chevalet.

CORDES ÉTOUFFÉES : Un effet de percussion produit en posant à plat la main sur le manche sans relâcher, puis en jouant les cordes avec le médiator.

NOTE: La vitesse des tirés est indiquée par la notation musicale et le tempo.

Erläuterung zur Tabulaturschreibweise

Es gibt drei Möglichkeiten, Gitarrenmusik zu notieren: im klassichen Notensystem, in Tabulaturform oder als rhythmische Akzente.

RHYTHMISCHE AKZENTE werden über dem Notensystem notiert. Geschlagene Akkorde werden rhythmisch dargestellt. Ausgeschriebene Noten stellen Einzeltöne dar.

Im **NOTENSYSTEM** werden Tonhöhe und rhythmischer Verlauf festgelegt; es ist durch Taktstriche in Takte unterteilt. Die Töne werden nach den ersten acht Buchstaben des Alphabets benannt.
Beachte: "B" in der anglo-amerkanischen Schreibweise entspricht dem deutschen "H"!

DIE TABULATUR ist die optische Darstellung des Gitarrengriffbrettes. Jeder horizontalen Linie ist eine bestimmte Saite zugeordnet, jede Zahl bezeichnet einen Bund.

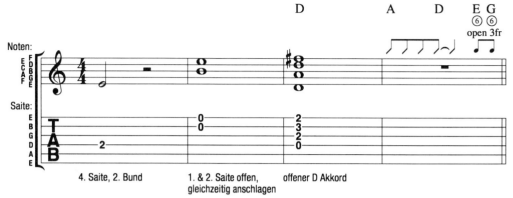

4. Saite, 2. Bund   1. & 2. Saite offen, gleichzeitig anschlagen   offener D Akkord

Erklärungen zur speziellen Gitarennotation

HALBTON-ZIEHER: Spiele die Note und ziehe dann um einen Halbton höher (Halbtonschritt).

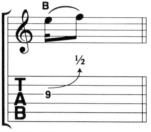

GANZTON-ZIEHER: Spiele die Note und ziehe dann einen Ganzton höher (Ganztonschritt).

ZIEHER MIT VORSCHLAG: Spiele die Note und ziehe wie notiert. Spiele die erste Note so schnell wie möglich.

VIERTELTON-ZIEHER: Spiele die Note und ziehe dann einen Viertelton höher (Vierteltonschritt).

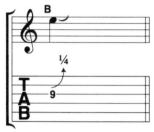

ZIEHEN UND ZURÜCKGLEITEN: Spiele die Note und ziehe wie notiert; lasse den Finger dann in die Ausgangposition zurückgleiten. Dabei wird nur die erste Note angeschlagen.

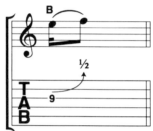

ZIEHEN UND NOCHMALIGES ANSCHLAGEN: Spiele die Note und ziehe wie notiert, schlage die Saite neu an, wenn das Symbol "▶" erscheint und lasse den Finger dann zurückgleiten.

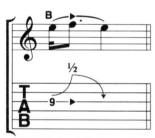

ZIEHER VOR DEM ANSCHLAGEN: Ziehe zuerst die Note wie notiert; schlage die Note dann an.

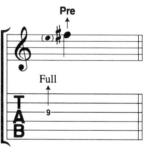

ZIEHER VOR DEM ANSCHLAGEN MIT ZURÜCKGLEITEN: Ziehe die Note wie notiert; schlage die Note dann an und lasse den Finger auf die Ausgangslage zurückgleiten.

AUFSCHLAGTECHNIK: Schlage die erste (tiefere) Note an; die höhere Note (auf der selben Saite) erklingt durch kräftiges Aufschlagen mit einem anderen Finger der Griffhand.

ABZIEHTECHNIK: Setze beide Finger auf die zu spielenden Noten und schlage die erste Note an. Ziehe dann (ohne nochmals anzuschlagen) den oberen Finger der Griffhand seitlich - abwärts ab, um die zweite (tiefere) Note zum klingen zu bringen.

GLISSANDOTECHNIK: Schlage die erste Note an und rutsche dann mit dem selben Finger der Griffhand aufwärts oder abwärts zur zweiten Note. Die zweite Note wird nicht angeschlagen.

GLISSANDOTECHNIK MIT NACHFOLGENDEM ANSCHLAG: Gleiche Technik wie das gebundene Glissando, jedoch wird die zweite Note angeschlagen.

NATÜRLICHES FLAGEOLETT: Berühre die Saite über dem angegebenen Bund leicht mit einem Finger der Griffhand. Schlage die Saite an und lasse sie frei schwingen.

PICK SCRAPE: Fahre mit dem Plektrum nach unten über die Saiten - klappt am besten bei umsponnenen Saiten.

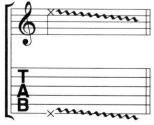

DÄMPFEN MIT DER SCHLAGHAND: Lege die Schlaghand oberhalb der Brücke leicht auf die Saite(n).

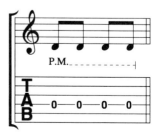

DÄMPFEN MIT DER GRIFFHAND: Du erreichst einen percussiven Sound, indem du die Griffhand leicht über die Saiten legst (ohne diese herunterzudrücken) und dann mit der Schlaghand anschlägst.

AMMERKUNG: Das Tempo der Zieher und Glissandos ist abhängig von der rhythmischen Notation und dem Grundtempo.

Spiegazioni Di Tablatura Per Chitarra

La musica per chitarra può essere annotata in tre diversi modi: sul pentagramma, in tablatura e in taglio ritmico

IL TAGLIO RITMICO è scritto sopra il pentagramma. Percuotere le corde al ritmo indicato Le teste arrotondate delle note indicano note singole.

IL PENTAGRAMMA MUSICALE mostra toni e ritmo ed è divisa da linee in settori. I toni sono indicati con le prime sette lettere dell'alfabeto.

LA TABLATURA rappresenta graficamente la tastiera della chitarra. Ogni linea orizzontale rappresenta una corda, ed ogni corda rappresenta un tasto.

4° corda, 2° tasto   1° e 2° corda aperte, suonate insieme   accordo D aperto

Definizioni Per Annotazioni Speciali Per Chitarra

SEMI-TONO CURVATO: percuotere la nota e curvare di un semitono (1/2 passo).

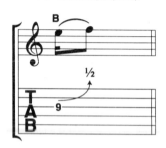

TONO CURVATO: Percuotere la nota e curvare di un tono (passo intero).

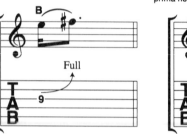

NOTA BREVE, CURVATA: percuotere la nota e curvare come indicato. Suonare la prima nota il più velocemente possibile.

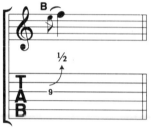

QUARTO DI TONO, CURVATO: Percuotere la nota e curvare di un quarto di passo.

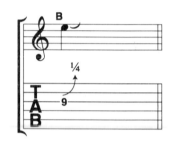

CURVA E LASCIA: Percuotere la nota e curvare come indicato, quindi rilasciare indietro alla nota originale.

CURVA E RIPERCUOTI: Percuotere la nota e curvare come indicato poi ripercuotere la corda nel punto del simbolo.

PRE-CURVA: Curvare la nota come indicato e quindi percuoterla.

PRE-CURVA E RILASCIO: Curvare la nota come indicato. Colpire e rilasciare la nota indietro alla tonalità indicata.

MARTELLO-COLPISCI: Colpire la prima nota (in basso) con un dito; quindi suona la nota più alta (sulla stessa corda) con un altro dito, toccandola senza pizzicare.

TOGLIERE: Posizionare entrambe le dita sulla nota da suonare. Colpire la prima nota e, senza pizzicare, togliere le dita per suonare la seconda nota (più in basso).

LEGATO SCIVOLATO (GLISSATO): Colpire la prima nota e quindi far scivolare lo stesso dito della mano della tastiera su o giù alla seconda nota. La seconda nota non viene colpita.

CAMBIO SCIVOLATO (GLISSARE E RICOLPIRE): Uguale al legato - scivolato eccetto che viene colpita la seconda nota.

ARMONICA NATURALE: Colpire la nota mentre la mano della tastiera tocca leggermente la corda direttamente sopra il tasto indicato.

PIZZICA E GRAFFIA: Il limite del pizzicato è tirato su (o giù) lungo la corda, producendo un suono graffiante.

SORDINA CON IL PALMO: La nota è parzialmente attenuato dalla mano del pizzicato toccando la corda (le corde) appena prima del ponte.

CORDE SMORZATE: Un suono di percussione viene prodotto appoggiando la mano della tastiera attraverso la corda (le corde) senza premere, e colpendole con la mano del pizzicato.

NOTA: La velocità di ogni curvatura è indicata dalle annotazioni musicali e dal tempo.

Printed in Great Britain by CPI Bath

1/04(50907)